CHINA
the culture

Bobbie Kalman

A Bobbie Kalman Book

The Lands, Peoples, and Cultures Series

 Crabtree Publishing Company
www.crabtreebooks.com

The Lands, Peoples, and Cultures Series
Created by Bobbie Kalman

Written by
Bobbie Kalman

Editors/first edition
Janine Schaub
Christine Arthurs
Margaret Hoogeveen

Revisions and updates
Plan B Book Packagers
Redbud Editorial

Coordinating Editor
Ellen Rodger

Proofreader
Adrianna Morganelli

Illustrations
Halina Below-Spada: p. 6, 18, 30
Dianne Eastman: icons
Tina Holdcroft: p. 24-25
David Wysotski, Allure Illustrations: back cover

Photographs
Afaizal/Shutterstock Inc.: p. 22; Jim Bryant: p. 10 (both); Sam Chadwick/Shutterstock Inc.: p. 1; Norman Chan/Shutterstock Inc.: p. 24; Dennis Cox/ChinaStock: p. 7 (top two), p. 8 (bottom right), p. 12 (top), p. 21 (top), p. 28 (top); David Butz p. 27 (bottom); Jordi Espel/Shutterstock Inc.: p. 5 (top left); Chee Choon Fat/Shutterstock Inc.: p. 9 (top), p. 25; Kim D. French/Shutterstock Inc.: p. 21 (bottom); Christine Gonsalves/Shutterstock Inc.: p. 16 (bottom); Luisa Fernanda Gonzalez/Shutterstock Inc.: p. 5 (bottom), p. 6; Lim Yong Hian/Shutterstock Inc.: p. 11 (bottom); Wolfgang Kaehler: p. 7 (bottom two), p. 17 (bottom); Kelvin Kho/Shutterstock Inc.: p. 11 (top); Postnikova Kristina/Shutterstock Inc.: p. 14 (bottom); Grigory Kubatyan/Shutterstock Inc.: p. 17 (top); Timur Kulgarin/Shutterstock Inc.: p. 29 (top); Christopher Liu/ChinaStock: p. 4, p. 15, p. 23, p. 27 (top), p. 29 (bottom); Ivanka Lupenic: p. 14 (top); Gayle McDougall: p. 8 (top); Stuart Miles/Shutterstock Inc.: p. 26; Tan Wei Ming/Shutterstock Inc.: p. 31 (bottom); Regien Paassen/Shutterstock Inc.: p. 30 (bottom); Bas Rabeling/Shutterstock Inc.: p. 13 (top); Chen Wei Seng /Shutterstock Inc.: p. 5 (right); Chin Kit Sen/Shutterstock Inc.: p. 15 (bottom), p. 23 (bottom); Gina Smith/Shutterstock Inc.: p. 19; Taolmor/Shutterstock Inc.: p. 30 (top); Khramtsova Tatyana/Shutterstock Inc.: p. 16 (top); Charles Taylor/Shutterstock Inc.: p. 18; Harald Høiland Tjøstheim/Shutterstock Inc.: p. 9 (bottom); Stephane Tougard/Shutterstock Inc.: p. 31 (top); Marc Verdiesen/Shutterstock Inc.: p. 28 (bottom); Teng Wei/Shutterstock Inc.: p. 13 (bottom); Tito Wong/Shutterstock Inc.: p. 12 (bottom); Liu Xiaoyang/China Stock: p. 20; other images by Digital Stock.

Every effort has been made to obtain the appropriate credit and full copyright clearance for all images in this book. Any oversights or omissions will be corrected in future editions.

Cover: A Peking Opera performer in dramatic makeup backstage at Beijing's Chang 'an Theater.

Title page: Dressed in yellow, members of a band pause during a lunar New Year parade. Chinese lunar New Year is a spectacular celebration with parades, fireworks, and special foods.

Back cover: The giant panda lives in the bamboo forests and mountain regions of southwestern China.

Library and Archives Canada Cataloguing in Publication

Kalman, Bobbie, 1947-
    China : the culture / Bobbie Kalman. -- 3rd ed., rev.

(Lands, peoples, and cultures series)
Includes index.
ISBN 978-0-7787-9301-4 (bound).--ISBN 978-0-7787-9669-5 (pbk.)

     1. China--Social life and customs--1976-2002--Juvenile literature.
I. Title. II. Series.

DS721.K35 2008   j951   C2007-907636-X

3MBL0000115428

Library of Congress Cataloging-in-Publication Data

Kalman, Bobbie.
    China. The culture / Bobbie Kalman. -- 3rd. ed., rev. ed.
      p. cm. -- (Lands, peoples, and cultures)
    "A Bobbie Kalman Book."
    Includes index.
    ISBN-13: 978-0-7787-9301-4 (rlb)
    ISBN-10: 0-7787-9301-X (rlb)
    ISBN-13: 978-0-7787-9669-5 (pb)
    ISBN-10: 0-7787-9669-8 (pb)
    1. China--Civilization--Juvenile literature. I. Title.
DS721.K1713 2008
951--dc22
                     2007051340

Crabtree Publishing Company
www.crabtreebooks.com   1-800-387-7650

Printed in the U.S.A./022011/WW20110117

Published in Canada
Crabtree Publishing
616 Welland Ave.
St. Catharines, ON
L2M 5V6

Published in the United States
Crabtree Publishing
PMB 59051
350 Fifth Avenue, 59th Floor
New York, New York 10118

Published in the United Kingdom
Crabtree Publishing
Maritime House
Basin Road North, Hove
BN41 1WR

Published in Australia
Crabtree Publishing
386 Mt. Alexander Rd.
Ascot Vale (Melbourne)
VIC 3032

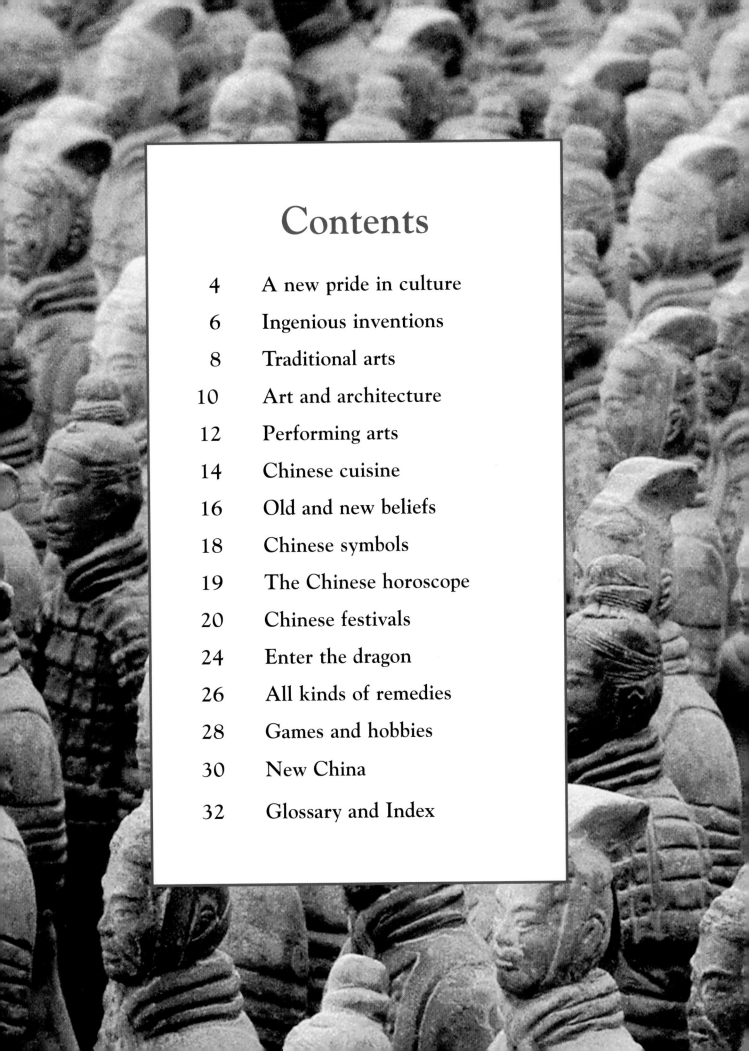

Contents

4 A new pride in culture

6 Ingenious inventions

8 Traditional arts

10 Art and architecture

12 Performing arts

14 Chinese cuisine

16 Old and new beliefs

18 Chinese symbols

19 The Chinese horoscope

20 Chinese festivals

24 Enter the dragon

26 All kinds of remedies

28 Games and hobbies

30 New China

32 Glossary and Index

A new pride in culture

The people of China have experienced a tremendous period of change in the last 100 years. During this period of political turmoil they had little time or energy for cultural activities. Sometimes people were fighting in wars to save their country. In the mid-1900s the government in power discouraged and even outlawed activities such as painting, dancing, playing music, and religious worship. People were punished for having an interest in arts that did not have government approval. This period of cultural **oppression** was known as the **Cultural Revolution**.

In the last few decades, China's culture has experienced a revival. People are rediscovering their **traditions**. They are once again celebrating traditional festivals and practicing their chosen religions. Painters, musicians, and writers all over the country are busy creating new works. The people of China are experiencing a renewed love for their arts and a new pride in their culture. They are also adopting new cultural practices that have their roots in other cultures.

These colorfully dressed citizens are celebrating the Chinese New Year.

(above) The dragon is an ancient symbol of China. The Chinese believe dragons are powerful and good.

(right) Beijing Opera, or jingxi, features colorful performers in roles with distinctive speaking, singing, and acrobatic roles. Men often dress as women in face paint.

(below) A colorful New Year flower decoration.

Ancient China's culture was more advanced than that of any other country. In those days Europeans had never seen creations such as the ones invented by the Chinese. Adventurers and merchants sailed to China to bring these treasured objects back to their countries. The clock, printing press, compass, wheelbarrow, crossbow, and animal harness, as well as **porcelain**, ink, and playing cards are just a few of the inventions the Chinese have passed on to the rest of the world.

Mulberry bark paper

In ancient China written records were kept on strips of bamboo that were tied together. These documents were difficult to store because they took up too much room. In 105 A.D., Ts'ai Lun, an official with the imperial court, had an ingenious idea. He made a mushy mixture of mulberry bark, **hemp**, rags, water, and old fishing nets. He pressed the pulp into a thin sheet and allowed it to dry. The result was the first piece of paper. Today, paper in China is sometimes made of bamboo, a renewable plant resource that is grown in forests.

Exploding bamboo

The first fireworks were made by stuffing gunpowder into hollow sticks of bamboo. Gunpowder is thought to have been discovered by accident—by medicine men who were trying to invent new cures for illness. The Chinese people adopted the use of gunpowder as a way to scare off evil spirits and ghosts. Fireworks are still used throughout China during festivals and holidays.

Paper lanterns are a Chinese invention. They are beautiful and useful too.

The compass

The Chinese were the first to discover that a magnetic object could indicate direction by pointing in a north-south direction. In ancient times, the Chinese used a **lodestone** to locate suitable burial sites. The lodestone was eventually replaced by a magnetized needle in a device called a compass.

The abacus

In China, students and businesspeople have traditionally used an abacus for making calculations. An abacus is a hand-operated device that consists of rows of beads on metal rods set in a rectangular wooden frame. The Chinese invented this counting instrument in the second century B.C.

Guarding the secret of silk

China has long been known for its beautiful silk material. Silk was transported and traded along a camel caravan route called the Silk Road, that ran through China and the mountains of Asia. For many years, the Chinese kept the secret of silk production to themselves. They knew that silk was made from the cocoons of tiny silkworms. The Chinese are still famous for the quality and beauty of their silk fabrics.

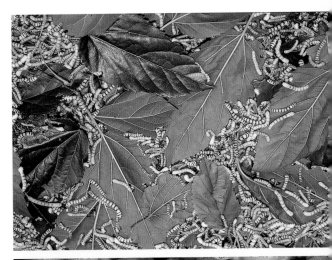

How silk is made

Producing silk is a lengthy process. It takes 40,000 silkworms to produce just twelve pounds (5.5 kg) of silk! The pictures on this page show the steps of silk-making. Match the information below to the pictures.

- After silkworm eggs are hatched in a warm room, baby worms feed on mulberry leaves until they are very fat. Thousands of feeding worms are kept on trays that are stacked one on top of another.

- The silkworms feed until they have stored up energy to enter the cocoon stage. The worms produce a jelly-like substance in their silk glands, which hardens when it comes into contact with air. Silkworms use this substance to spin a cocoon around themselves.

- After eight or nine days in a warm, dry place the cocoons are ready to be unwound. First they are steamed or baked to kill the pupas, or worms. The cocoons are dipped into hot water to loosen the tightly woven strands. Then the strands are unwound onto a spool. Each cocoon is made up of a thread between 1,968 and 2,953 feet (600 and 900 m) long!

- The silk threads are woven into cloth or used for embroidery work. Clothes made from silk are not only beautiful and lightweight, they are also warm in cool weather and cool in hot weather!

Traditonal arts

The Chinese are famous for their traditional arts. Painting and calligraphy, sculpture, architecture, and the creation of fine porcelain are just a few of the arts that date far back into the history of Chinese culture.

Calligraphy

The art of fine writing is called calligraphy. The first great Chinese calligraphers lived 1,600 years ago. In ancient times, the Chinese people thought calligraphy to be the most beautiful art form. Artists were highly respected because it took great skill to master the difficult brushstrokes.

Delicate brushstrokes

Calligraphy is still important in modern China. When children learn to read and write, they also learn calligraphy's delicate brushstrokes. The thousands of complicated **pictographs** that make up the Chinese alphabet are based on the eight brushstrokes of calligraphy. The basic tools for calligraphy are called the four treasures. They are paper, ink, ink stone, and brush.

Calligraphers often write out poems in fine script using black ink and brushes made from animal hair. Chinese writing is well suited to poetry because many of its pictographs resemble the idea they are communicating. For example, the character for "way" or "path" looks something like a foot striding forward, as if a person were actually walking down a path.

(top) The scene pictured is part of a painted ceiling at the Summer Palace near Beijing. (above) A child practices Chinese writing.

8

This calligraphic symbol for the word outstanding, is painted on a golden background.

Painting

Traditional Chinese painting is based on the eight brushstrokes that are used in calligraphy. Many other brushstrokes are used as well, each with a certain purpose. For example, a particular stroke is used for painting bamboo, another for trees, and one for rocks and mountains. Many Chinese paintings depict nature. Landscapes and symbolic birds and flowers are popular subjects.

These works of art are painted on long panels of paper or silk. Fans, screens, and wall and ceiling panels are also painted. A painted handscroll made of silk or paper is read by slowly unrolling the scroll for viewers to see. A poem often accompanies the painting to help people understand the meaning of the picture.

Chinese porcelain

Pottery was one of the first crafts of ancient China. The finest of all pottery is porcelain, which the Chinese invented. Porcelain is made from a mixture of coal dust and a fine, white clay called kaolin. Chinese porcelain is fired at temperatures of more than 2100°F (1150°C). It is then glazed and fired again to make it shiny and hard. Chinese artists began using a deep blue dye made from a mineral called cobalt to create the beautiful blue-and-white vases made during the Ming dynasty. These vases became famous all over the world. Chinese porcelain was eventually in such great demand that merchants from many countries sailed to China for it and it became known as china. Today people use this term, not only for porcelain, but for all kinds of dishes and pottery.

This spectacular golden Buddha from a Chinese temple, is an example of ornate goldsmithing.

9

In ancient China, the ability to sculpt was considered a skill rather than an art. Great sculptures were created to express religious devotion. Images of **Buddha** carved out of natural rock formations are among China's most spectacular works of art. Some of these carvings are as tall as five-story buildings.

Thousands of Buddhas

In clusters of caves in northern China, thousands of images of Buddha have been carved into the cave walls. The oldest of these are the Dunhuang Caves. Monks carved Buddhas and painted the walls there for over ten centuries. There are 492 caves containing more than 2,000 sculptures of the Buddha and many religious wall paintings. The Yungang Grottoes near Datong contain the largest and most beautiful cave sculptures in China. Although many caves have been deteriorating, fifty-three of them survive, containing over 50,000 images of the Buddha.

Some of China's cave Buddhas are so lifelike that they are nicknamed the "living rock."

(right) Monks painted images of the angels, symbols, and animals on cave walls next to sculptures of the Buddha.

Traditional architecture

Chinese civilization is thousands of years old, but only a few ancient buildings are still standing. Most of China's early buildings were made of wood, which has decayed over time. Wood was used to build homes and temples because the Chinese liked its natural qualities. The oldest building in China is a wooden temple built in the year 782. Colorful buildings with curved, upswept eaves, bright roof tiles, and carved adornments are all part of traditional Chinese architecture. The dragon, crane, phoenix, unicorn, and other symbols are painted or carved into the walls and roof supports. These animals symbolize good fortune and long life.

Meaning in architecture

The way buildings are constructed and decorated has meaning in Chinese culture. Red is used to bring good fortune, and yellow is the emperor's color. The number of steps or columns usually represents important things such as the four seasons of the year. The Chinese use a set of principles called *feng shui* to determine how their buildings can be in harmony with the surrounding environment to bring them good fortune. For example, buildings face south because north is thought to be the source of evil.

Pretty pagodas

Pagodas look like several one-story buildings stacked on top of one another, with each story having its own roof. The highest ones are the most sacred. Pagodas can be found at Buddhist temples and contain religious relics. They are not designed as dwellings. In fact, they usually have solid cores!

Ornamented architecture, with swooping roofs and decorative columns, is a common traditional style in China.

The Temple of Heaven in Beijing was constructed between 1406 and 1420 and was used for annual "good harvest" ceremonies.

Amazing circus acrobats

Imagine trying to balance another person on your head while standing on top of a stack of ten chairs! Acrobats must be very agile and flexible to perform stunts such as spinning plates on tall poles or juggling while walking on a giant ball. For 2,000 years, professional Chinese acrobats have been performing these difficult and spectacular tricks. Today, acrobatic and circus troupes continue to amaze audiences throughout China and around the world.

A night at the opera

The opera is a popular form of entertainment in China. Operas are at least three hours long. At one time they lasted up to three days! Although the songs in a Chinese opera may be hard to understand, even for someone who speaks Chinese, the viewer can still understand what is going on from the gestures, makeup, and costumes. A trembling body, for example, means fear, and crossed eyes show anger. The villain always has a white patch on his nose. There are many different styles of opera, each one originating from a different region. Of all the styles, the most famous is the Beijing Opera, or *jingxi*. It features high-pitched singing, elaborate costumes, and a large **percussion** section. Beijing operas are often based on historical events.

(top and bottom) Chinese opera singers wear elaborate costumes and makeup.

Acrobatics

Acrobatics is a popular form of entertainment in China. Chinese acrobatics originated from ancient martial arts performances where competitors showed their skills with weapons. Today, Chinese acrobats are known throughout the world for their flexibility and daring. Many acrobats train in Chinese circuses and Chinese films show off the amazing talents of actors who seem to be able to walk through air, on water, and through the tops of trees. Often it is acrobatic skill and **guywires** that help them perform such feats.

Chinese music

When the **Cultural Revolution** came to an end, the Chinese government started encouraging people to take up cultural activities such as music once again. Although western music is popular in China now, the Chinese also have great pride in their traditional music. Traditional music dates back thousands of years when music was a part of royal court activities. People all over China attend concerts in which typical Chinese instruments, such as the *hu qin*, the *pipa* lute, and *sheng* pipes are played. Modern Chinese pop music is very popular, and pop stars have huge fan bases. Some are also film stars. Jackie Chan, for instance, has released twenty pop albums in over twenty years.

(top) An acrobat performs an exercise with a tray of glasses balanced on her foot.

(bottom) Film star Jackie Chan was born in Hong Kong and trained in drama, martial arts, and acrobatics before launching his movie career.

Chinese cooking is known for its variety of flavors and textures and by its many different cooking styles. Steaming and stir-frying are the most common ways to cook food in China. In China, chefs are so highly regarded for their cooking skills that they are sometimes called "doctors of food."

Fresh and fast

Chinese food is prepared with the freshest ingredients. Bite-sized pieces cook quickly and can be eaten easily with chopsticks. Stir-frying food in a wok is one of the most popular cooking methods. Only a small amount of oil is needed in this deep, round frying pan. Chinese cooks do not like to waste anything. Whether from land or sea, almost every type and part of an animal is eaten, including eels, sea slugs, snakes, and chicken feet.

Regional cooking styles

There are five major styles of Chinese cooking: Canton, Fukien, Honan, Sichuan, and Shantung. The Cantonese style originates from the region around Guangzhou (once known as Canton) and is the most familiar to Westerners. Dishes such as egg rolls, chop suey, and chow mein are all part of Cantonese cooking. A mild climate and access to the sea give the chefs of this area a wide variety of ingredients.

Fukien, Honan, and Sichuan

The province of Fukien has a long sea coast, so a wide variety of seafood is available to its residents. Fukien cuisine is well known for its delicate flavors and clear soups.

(above) A wok is used to prepare many Chinese dishes.

(below) Dried squid hangs on a clothespinned line. Seafood such as squid is popular in China.

(above) This family is sharing a Mongolian Hot Pot meal.

Cooks of Honan were the first to produce the famous Chinese sweet-and-sour sauce and the deep-fried method of cooking. Sichuan cooking is famous for spicy foods that can set your mouth on fire! Sichuan dishes are made with red chili and peppercorn pastes.

Shantung

The Shantung style of cooking comes from the north. It is best known for duck soup and Peking Duck. Peking Duck is a delicacy that comes from Beijing, which used to be known as Peking. The waiter announces the arrival of this fabulous dish at the table by striking a gong. Little rice is farmed in the north, so wheat noodles and dumplings serve as the northern residents' staple starchy foods.

The Mongolian Hot Pot

The Mongolian Hot Pot came to China during the time the **Mongols** ruled the country. It is a famous northern fondue-style meal that is centered around a pot filled with boiling soup stock. A variety of raw meat is arranged in dishes around the pot. Diners cook by dipping pieces of meat into the boiling broth.

The meat cooks quickly and adds flavor to the boiling stock. Several sauces, such as hot mustard, peanut, and soya, go with the meat. After the diners have finished their meat, they drink the flavorful broth to which vegetables such as spinach and cabbage have been added.

Eating Chinese style

The traditional Chinese table is round to allow guests to be at an equal distance from the food. Each place setting has bowls, a spoon, sauces, and chopsticks. Dishes are brought in one at a time, and the diners serve themselves from a platter. When eating with chopsticks, never touch your mouth with the chopsticks and never cross your chopsticks when you have finished your meal. Both of these actions are considered bad manners.

All the tea in China

No Chinese meal is complete without a pot of hot tea. In fact, the Chinese introduced the rest of the world to this popular beverage. Tea is still an important part of Chinese culture. It is sipped at every meal, offered to all guests, and served in local teahouses.

(below) Bean paste moon cakes are served for dessert.

Chinese folk religion is filled with gods, demons, and spirits. Many of China's traditional festivals are based on ancient **myths**.

Yin and *Yang*

Many Chinese believe that the universe is made up of two forces: *yin* and *yang*. *Yin* is feminine and *yang* is masculine. *Yin* and *yang* are opposites that work together to create a balance. The well-being of the world, the body, and the soul are believed to depend on these forces staying in balance.

The teachings of Confucius

Confucius was a **scholar** who lived from 551 to 479 B.C. He introduced a code by which many Chinese people lived. Confucius said the ideal person was polite, honest, courageous, and wise. For more than 2,000 years Chinese society followed the Confucian code. Children were taught to obey, and everyone was expected to respect the elderly and obey the rulers.

Laotzu and Taoism

Taoism is also very old. It is based on a short book called the *Tao te Ching*, written by a man known as Laotzu, who lived around the same time as Confucius. Taoists believe that achieving the balance of the *yin* and *yang* is the key to achieving spiritual peace. Taoism teaches the importance of harmony with nature and encourages a simple way of life. Both Confucianism and Taoism have deeply affected the characters of the Chinese people over the centuries.

(top right) Yin *is characterized as soft, right, and cold and* Yang *as hard, left, and warm.*

(left) The Chinese sometimes worship their ancestors, who are thought to possess the power to help or hinder living descendants.

Buddhism

Centuries ago, a man named Sakyamuni lived in India. One day while meditating, he discovered the meaning of life and how to end the suffering of all people. He became the Buddha, which means the "Awakened One." Those who follow his teachings believe that people are born over and over again as human beings, animals, or insects. If you do good deeds in this life, your next life will be a good one. But if you live a life of evil, your next life will be full of misfortune. **Buddhism** came to China from India in the fifth century B.C. Over the years China has developed its own version called Chan Buddhism, or Zen Buddhism.

Islam and Christianity

Islam was founded at Mecca, Saudi Arabia, by a **prophet** named Muhammed. It was brought to China by Arab traders in the seventh century. The Kazaks and Uygurs who live in the western regions follow the Islamic faith. Christianity, which is based on the teachings of Jesus Christ, was introduced to China in the sixteenth century by European **missionaries**.

Freedom to believe?

China's government does not tolerate religions or beliefs that it sees as a challenge to **Communist** authority. For this reason, some people are **persecuted**. The government banned the Falun Gong belief system in 1999. Falun Gong has its roots in traditional Chinese folk religion and teaches truthfulness and compassion. Falun Gong has millions of followers. The Chinese government thinks Falun Gong is a threat to its power and has imprisoned many followers of Falun Gong.

(above) Colorful Muslim prayer caps in Xinjiang.

(below) A golden Buddha statue sits at the front of a temple. In 1982, the Chinese government allowed its citizens to worship freely, but not all belief systems are tolerated.

Over the centuries the Chinese have created many symbols to express the values that are important to them. Signs, colors, and even animals symbolize such things as long life, happiness, peace, and beauty.

Shou — The *shou* sign was adapted from the Chinese character or pictograph that means long life. It appears everywhere—sewn onto silk, carved in jade, and painted on porcelain.

Fu — The sign for happiness also comes from the Chinese language. The character *fu* is often surrounded by bats because *fu* also means bat.

Dragon — The dragon is a symbol representing the country of China, rain, and spring. According to an ancient Chinese legend, the dragon was the god of rain. Clouds formed when the dragon breathed. In spring the dragon brought the rain; in winter the dragon buried itself in the mud at the bottom of the sea. The dragon is a symbol of new life.

Phoenix — The phoenix is an imaginary bird that looks something like a peacock. It is a symbol of beauty, peace, the summer harvest, and long life. When pictured together, the dragon and phoenix foretell good luck, so they are often used as wedding decorations.

Unicorn — The Chinese unicorn looks different from the ones you may have seen in pictures. The unicorn is a Buddhist symbol of wisdom, so it is sometimes shown carrying a law book.

Tortoise — The tortoise is a symbol of the universe. Its round back represents the sky, and its belly the earth. The tortoise is a symbol of strength and long life because it was believed to live for a thousand years.

Lion — Sculptures of lions are often placed as guards outside important buildings. A male lion is usually shown playing with a ball. A female lion has a tiny cub under her paw.

The Chinese horoscope

The year of the dog

Astrology is the study of how the stars and planets relate to a person's fortune and well-being. The ancient Chinese horoscope predicts that people born in a certain year have a particular set of characteristics. A Chinese legend tells the story of a time when all the animals of the world were invited to come and visit the Buddha. Only twelve animals came. In order to reward these animals for their loyalty, the Buddha named a year after each one in the order they appeared before him. The cycle of animal names repeats every twelve years. The people born in the year of a certain animal are believed to have some of the characteristics of that animal. Check the chart below for your sign.

Your year

Year of the Rat
1960, 1972, 1984, 1996, 2008

Year of the Ox
1961, 1973, 1985, 1997, 2009

Year of the Tiger
1962, 1974, 1986, 1998, 2010

Year of the Rabbit
1963, 1975, 1987, 1999, 2011

Year of the Dragon
1964, 1976, 1988, 2000, 2012

Year of the Snake
1965, 1977, 1989, 2001, 2013

Year of the Horse
1954, 1966, 1978, 1990, 2002

Year of the Sheep
1955, 1967, 1979, 1991, 2003

Year of the Monkey
1956, 1968, 1980, 1992, 2004

Year of the Rooster
1957, 1969, 1981, 1993, 2005

Year of the Dog
1958, 1970, 1982, 1994, 2006

Year of the Boar
1959, 1971, 1983, 1995, 2007

Are these your traits?

- You are charming, fussy, and a penny pincher. Only through love will you become generous.
- You are quiet and patient until angered. You inspire confidence. You are also stubborn.
- You are courageous. Sometimes you are selfish. Though sympathetic, you can be suspicious.
- You are fortunate and well-respected. Sometimes you are a daydreamer.
- You are healthy, energetic, short-tempered, and stubborn. You are honest and brave.
- You are quiet and wise and like to dress up. You help other people but tend to overdo it.
- You are independent. You talk too much. You are popular but sometimes you trust the wrong people.
- You are gentle in your ways. Sometimes you are pessimistic. You are a very cultured person.
- You are a genius, but you are not steady. Though clever and skillful, you can be impatient.
- Only sometimes are you fortunate. You work hard, but you often take on too much.
- You have a deep sense of loyalty and duty. Your tongue is sharp, but you keep secrets well.
- You are brave and can do anything you decide to do. You have few friends, but they last for life.

Chinese festivals

In China, many festivals are connected with national celebrations. Labor Day, Women's Day, and Children's Day are just a few of these. The most important celebrations in modern China are Liberation Day and Chinese New Year.

National Day

On October 1, 1949, **Mao Zedong** announced the founding of the People's Republic of China. National Day is now celebrated every year on October 1. It is the biggest national holiday in China. People from all over the country gather in Beijing to take part in a huge parade.

The lunar calendar

Chinese people use the **lunar** calendar to count the passing of years. This ancient calendar is based on the cycles of the moon. A month starts when the new moon appears in the sky. According to the lunar calendar, one year has thirteen months.

People wave banners and march past the Gate of Heavenly Peace on National Day. After the parade, thousands go to the **Forbidden City** for fireworks, singing, and dancing.

Spring Festival

Chinese New Year, also known as the Spring Festival, falls in early spring. The Chinese New Year is held on the first day of the first lunar month, which occurs at the end of January or beginning of February. The celebrations last for an entire week. An ancient Chinese legend says that a long time ago, there was a monster who ate people. The gods decided to lock him up inside a mountain to protect people. Once a year during New Year, the gods allowed him to come out. The Chinese kept him away from their homes by lighting firecrackers. This bright, noisy display has become a tradition at midnight every New Year.

(below) ***The dragon dance helps ring in the Chinese New Year.***

20

Making preparations

Spring Festival is a big celebration, and everyone prepares for the event well in advance. People begin by setting up an altar for Zao Wang, the lord of the stove. At one time a picture of Zao Wang hung by the kitchen stove in every home. People believed that he went up to heaven during the Spring Festival and reported to the gods about each household. If the report was good, the gods would look after the family throughout the rest of the year. To make sure Zao Wang had sweet things to say, the Chinese spread honey on his mouth! Before the New Year arrives, people pay back debts and rid their hearts of grudges toward others.

A family time

During Spring Festival, families visit the tombs of their dead relatives. They honor their ancestors by lighting **incense** and burning imitation money. Afterwards, they go back to their homes for a huge feast. Children are given little red packets filled with money, and their parents let them stay up late.

(above) These children in Inner Mongolia wear bright clothes to celebrate the Naadam festival.

Dancing dragons

On the third day of the Spring Festival there is a parade of dragon and lion dancers. The dragon costume has a papier-mâché head and a long, colorful, sequin-covered body. The dragon is so huge, it takes two people to hold up its head and twelve more to act as its legs. The streets are full of people. As the dragon passes people's homes, they open their doors to let in the good luck that the dragon brings.

(below) The Lantern Festival comes after Chinese New Year.

Traditional and modern

In China, people celebrate festivals that date back to ancient times. Although many traditional festivals were replaced by national festivals at the beginning of the Cultural Revolution, people in **rural** areas often continued to celebrate in the old ways. Most traditional festivals correspond to important dates on the old Chinese calendar.

Harvest Moon Festival

Food is important to everyone, so celebrating the harvest is one of the most important holidays around the world. It is no different in China. The Chinese celebrate this special time of thanksgiving with the Harvest Moon Festival. On the evening of the Harvest Moon Festival, people climb hills and mountains to get a good view of the full moon. They carry fish- and bird-shaped paper lanterns. They give thanks for the harvest to the bright full moon of the eighth lunar month. Sometimes people also burn moon papers which have pictures of rabbits and toads.

According to Chinese mythology, a rabbit and a three-legged toad live on the moon. They are the moon's companions.

Sweet moon cakes

On the eve of the festival, friends and relatives give each other pastries called moon cakes. These small cakes contain a variety of sweet fillings, such as almond paste, red bean paste, or eggs. An old legend recounts how moon cakes once saved the Chinese. A long time ago, China was ruled by people from foreign countries. The Chinese wanted the foreigners to leave the country. At the Harvest Moon Festival they hid messages inside moon cakes and passed them around to let everyone know of a secret plan to gain back control of China. At the arranged time, they gathered together and succeeded in overthrowing their cruel rulers.

These dragon heads will be worn in a parade marking the Harvest Moon Festival.

During the Harvest Moon Festival, family and friends gather together to celebrate the harvest. They eat many delicious treats, including traditional pastries called moon cakes.

Harvest moon cookies

Harvest moon cakes are difficult to make, but you can make our version of harvest moon cookies instead! Here are the ingredients you will need for the cookie dough:

1 cup (250 mL) softened butter
1/2 cup (125 mL) icing sugar
2 tsp (10 mL) vanilla
1 cup (250 mL) ground blanched almonds
1 1/2 cups (375 mL) sifted all-purpose flour

Cream butter with a big spoon. Sift sugar and gradually mix with the butter. Blend in vanilla and almonds, and slowly knead in flour. Put dough into refrigerator for one hour.

The fun part

Once the dough is chilled, it is ready for rolling. Sprinkle some flour on your rolling pin and on the kitchen counter. Roll out your dough to a thickness of 1/3 of an inch (1 cm). Now you can cut or form it into shapes! An upside-down glass works well as a full-moon-shaped cookie cutter. Make a crescent-shaped moon by cutting a full moon into two halves and pulling at the two ends until it looks like a crescent shape. To make a rabbit or a toad, cut the shapes out on a piece of paper, press the paper down on the rolled-out dough, and trim around the shape. Bake the cookies on a greased cookie sheet in a preheated 350°F (180°C) oven for fifteen minutes.

There many other traditional Chinese festivals and most of them feature the dragon in some way. The dragon is an icon of China and traditionally, the Chinese are said to be descendants of the dragon. Some festivals feature giant dragons made from lanterns, and other include dragons in parades and boat races.

Lantern Festival

The Lantern Festival comes two weeks after the Spring Festival. During this celebration people carry candlelit lanterns shaped like dragons and other Chinese icons, including goldfish, birds, and red globes. Sometimes groups of children perform a lantern dance.

Qing Ming Festival

The Qing Ming Festival takes place in April. It is a time when Chinese people honor the dead. People tend the graves of deceased relatives with great care. The family often shares a picnic lunch and burns sticks of incense in honor of their ancestors. Over the years, the festival has also come to honor those who fought and died in the revolutionary war.

The Dragon Boat Festival

The Dragon Boat Festival is celebrated in southern China. It is held in remembrance of the politician and poet Qu Yuan. In 288 B.C., Qu Yuan ended his life by throwing himself into the Miluo River in Hunan Province to protest the corrupt government. People respected Qu Yuan and wanted to find him and give him a proper funeral and burial.

People launched their boats and threw rice dumplings into the river to distract the fish from his body while they searched for him.

Boat racing

Today, people eat rice dumplings and race boats shaped like dragons to honor Qu Yuan's memory. Dragon boats are long and slim, sometimes over eighty-nine feet (27 m) long. The **prow** is carved in the shape of a huge dragon head and the **hull** is beautifully painted. Up to seventy rowers are needed to power each boat. The spectators cheer for their favorite teams, clang cymbals and gongs, and wave colorful flags. The dragon boat race is a noisy and exciting festival!

(opposite) A brilliant dragon painting from the wall of a Chinese temple.

(below) Dragon boat racers light a paper dragon before the start of a race.

The Chinese practice modern western medicine, but they also follow traditional Chinese methods for curing illness. These ancient healing techniques are 6,000 years old. Patients are treated with massage, medicinal herbs, acupuncture, exercise, and cupping.

Restoring the balance

Many Chinese people believe that illness is caused by an interruption in the *chi*, which is the vital energy of the body. Just as the *yin* and *yang* create a balance in the universe, these forces must also be balanced in the body so that the *chi* can flow properly. When the body is out of balance, a person becomes ill. A person with too much heat in his or her body, for example, might suffer from boils. Since heat is caused by the *yang*, the doctor will prescribe a *yin* remedy such as dandelions, which have a cooling effect.

Hundreds of remedies line the shelves of this herbalist's shop.

Herbs and "dragon bones"

Treatment with medicinal herbs is the most popular kind of traditional Chinese medicine. A well-stocked herbalist carries up to 6,000 remedies. Wood, bark, and ten types of ginseng root are used as herbal-tea ingredients. Ground up animal parts, such as seashells and fossilized bones and teeth, known as "dragon bones," are also used as remedies.

Cures that kill animals

Each year, thousands of animals are killed to meet the demand for Chinese medical supplies. Some herbalists sell bear paws, rhinoceros horns, deer antlers, and sea horses. Some of these animals are **endangered species**. Hunters sometimes even kill pandas by accident while trying to trap other animals. There are only a thousand pandas left in the world! Poachers also hunt rhinoceroses, deer, tigers, and bears in other parts of the world such as Africa, India, and Canada. This practice angers many people.

The mystery of acupuncture

Acupuncture is an ancient way of treating illness by stimulating certain pressure points on the body. Thin, sterilized needles are painlessly inserted at key points on the body. Stimulating these points is said to balance the patient's *chi*. Acupuncture is used to cure ailments, relieve pain, and anesthetize patients for surgery. An anesthetic is a substance that causes a patient to lose feeling in a certain area of his or her body. When acupuncture is used as an anesthetic, patients remain awake throughout an operation and can even talk to the doctor.

Cupping

Cupping is another traditional technique used by Chinese doctors. Bamboo cups are immersed in hot water and are then applied to the body at acupuncture points. When the cup is put on the skin, the hot air inside cools and creates suction. The skin swells up into the cup as the blood beneath the surface rushes into the small surface vessels. Cupping is believed to relieve congestion caused by asthma, and the aches and pains that accompany many diseases.

Barefoot doctors

Barefoot doctors are not doctors without shoes. They are rural **paramedics** who are qualified to treat minor medical problems. They also educate people about health and personal hygiene. Barefoot doctors were once part-time rice farmers who worked in the fields in their bare feet, just like the other farmers. Now they are trained in both western and traditional medical techniques and work full time in clinics and country hospitals.

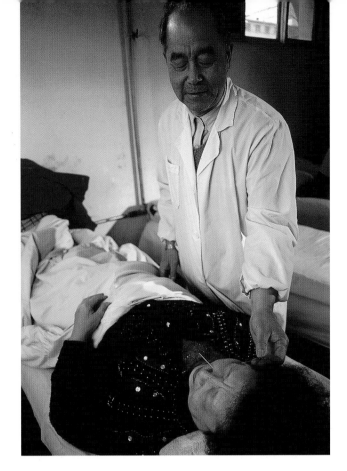

(above) A doctor inserts tiny needles into a patient as part of an acupuncture treatment.

(below) Dentists advertise their skills with illustrated signs in a Kashgar bazaar. Kashgar is located in Northwestern China.

The Chinese are passionate about their hobbies. Clusters of friends gather in the streets and parks to discuss their favorite pastimes. Many people can also be seen playing a variety of traditional games.

Mah jong

Mah jong is a popular adult game. People play it with great enthusiasm. *Mah jong* is similar to the card game Gin Rummy, but it has a set of 136 tiles rather than fifty-two cards. Instead of hearts, diamonds, spades, and clubs, *mah jong* tiles are decorated with bamboo, circles, and characters. The sound of *mah jong* being played is as distinctive as the game itself. The loud clicking of tiles being moved furiously around the table top is a familiar noise.

Chinese chess and checkers

Chinese chess is not the same as international chess. Like international chess, Chinese chess is played on a board and involves "taking" the opponent's pieces, but there are no knights, kings, or queens. Chinese chess is an ancient game.

It uses flat, round, black and white stones on a grid-patterned board. The Chinese watch large national chess tournaments with keen interest. They also have their own version of checkers played on a star-shaped board.

(above) Chinese checkers is played all over the world.

(below) Watching movies is a favorite pastime, as these movie posters for western and Chinese movies show.

Fancy footwork

One popular children's game is Kick-the Bag. To play this game, a little bag is sewn together and filled with sand or grain. Then it is thrown into the air and kicked over and over again with the inside of the heel. Kick-the-Bag can be played by one person or with others in a small circle. Another version of this game is called *ti jian zi*. Children find something light, such as a cork or a coin with a hole, and attach a feather to it for balance. They try to keep it in the air following rules similar to those of Kick-the-Bag. This game is far more difficult than it looks!

"Small games"

One of the best-loved hobbies in China is called "small games," or keeping pets. In China few families have a dog as a pet. Instead, people keep pigeons, singing birds, goldfish, and even crickets! In China, crickets have been kept as pets for thousands of years. Women at the imperial palace used to keep these singing insects in golden cages. Now, instead of golden cages, people use little bamboo baskets for their crickets. In winter, the owner puts a tiny hot-water bottle inside the basket to keep the cricket warm. Not only are crickets easy to feed, they are also easy to carry along in a pocket.

Some owners take their crickets to fighting matches that attract large audiences. The crickets are placed in a wooden bowl used as the fighting ring. Many Chinese also keep birds as pets. Elderly people often bring their songbirds to the park and hang their cages in the trees. Some people keep pigeons. Owners attach homemade whistles to their pigeons' tails. As the birds fly through the air, the wind causes the whistles to blow.

(above) A man practices his calligraphy in his home art studio.

(below) A young girl plays a game of **ti jian zi** *on the street outside of her Beijing home.*

China has changed rapidly over the last two decades. Economic policies introduced by the **Communist** government after 1979 have created booms in industry, trade, technology, and construction. China has a new **middle class** that has made economic **prosperity** as important as political freedoms. Many Chinese can now afford to buy the luxury items that their parents and grandparents never even dreamed about. China's **economy** has grown faster than any other country's economy because the government has welcomed private ownership and foreign investment. Private ownership in China is under the Communist government's watchful eye and control.

(top) Cranes load ships destined for Europe and the Americas, with consumer goods produced in Chinese factories.

(right) A woman sells Chinese flags to tourists at Tiananmen Square, the scene of a famous 1989 democracy protest.

30

Rich and poor

The new prosperity is not without its problems. China is one of the world's largest exporter of goods and has one of the biggest economies in the world. Chinese workers are fueling the economic boom in the country's cities but many rural Chinese are still poor. Many have left their villages for better paying jobs in the big cities. The Chinese people have more economic freedom than before, but no ability to elect their government.

Tiananmen legacy?

In 1989, thousands of Chinese, including students, staged a protest in Beijing's Tiananmen Square. The protest called for greater freedoms and democracy, or the right to elect their government. The Communist government put a stop to the protests with gunfire. Thousands were killed and many others were thrown in jail. In China today, there is no public discussion of the democracy protests at Tiananmen, but many people hope economic changes will lead to other freedoms in the future.

(above) A soldier stands guard beneath a portrait of former leader Mao Zedong near the entrance of Beijing's Forbidden City.

(below) A street in the business district of Suzhou, China bustles with shoppers eager to spend their new wealth.

Glossary

ancestors People from whom one is descended
Buddha An ancient religious leader from India
Buddhism A religion founded by Buddha
Communist Describing an economic system in which the country's resources are held in common by all the people and regulated by the government
Cultural Revolution A time of fear and terror in China from 1966-1971 when all things considered western were banned and many people were sent to jail
economy The financial resources of a country
endangered species A species of animal that is very close to becoming extinct
Forbidden City A public museum in Beijing. It was originally a palace built in the 15th century, which only government officials and members of the emperor's family could enter
guywires Wires or ropes designed to hold someone or something up in the air
hemp A strong plant fiber used to make rope
hull The bottom and sides of a ship
incense A substance that produces a sweet-smelling smoke when burned
lodestone A type of iron ore that is naturally magnetized and can be used to indicate direction
lunar Relating to the moon
Mao Zedong Founder of the Chinese Communist Party and China's leader for twenty-seven years
middle class A class of people between the rich and the poor

missionaries People sent by a church to spread their religion to those who do not believe in it
Mongol One of China's fifty-six national groups, who live in the autonomous region of Inner Mongolia
myth A legend or story that tries to explain mysterious events or ideas
oppression Power excercised over people in a brutal way
paramedic A trained medical worker capable of performing basic medical procedures
percussion Relating to musical instruments that require striking
persecute To harass or hurt someone because of their religion, race, or beliefs
pictograph A picture used to represent a word
prophet A religious leader believed to be inspired by God or a spirit
prosperity Being successful, especially in money matters
prow The front part of a boat
rural Relating to the countryside
scholar A person who devotes their life to the study of something
symbol Something that represents or stands for something else
Taoism A religion based on the teachings of Laotzu, an ancient Chinese philosopher
tradition A long-held custom or practice

 # Index

abacus 6
acrobats 12, 13
acupuncture 26, 27
architecture 8, 10-11
barefoot doctors 27
Buddha 9, 10, 17, 19
Buddhism 11, 17, 18
calligraphy 8, 9, 29
Chinese chess 28
chopsticks 14, 15
Confucious 16
cooking 14-15
crickets 29
Cultural Revolution 4, 22
cupping 26, 27
dancing 4, 20, 21, 22, 24
Dragon Boat Festival 24
dragons 5, 11, 18, 20, 21, 22, 24, 26
Dunhuang Caves 10
feng shui 11
festivals 4, 6, 16, 20-23, 24
fireworks 6, 20, 21
Forbidden City 20, 31
games and hobbies 28-29
harvest moon cakes 22, 23
Harvest Moon Festival 22, 23
herbs 26
horoscope 19
inventions 6-7
Islam 17
Lantern Festival 21, 24
Liberation Day 20
mah jong 28
Mao Zedong 20, 31
medicine 26-27
Mongols 15
music 4, 13
New Year 4, 5, 20, 21
opera 5, 12
pagodas 11
painting 4, 8, 9, 10, 24
paper 6, 9
pets 29
pipas 13
poetry 8, 9
porcelain 6, 8, 9
pottery 9
Qing Ming Festival 24
religions 4, 10, 11, 16, 17
sculptures 8, 10, 18
silk 7, 9
songbirds 29
Spring Festival 20, 21, 24
symbols 5, 11, 18
Taoism 16
tea 15
writing 4, 8, 9
yin and yang 16, 26